DISRUPTIVE THINKING

STUDY GUIDE

DISRUPTIVE THINKING

STUDY GUIDE

A DARING STRATEGY TO CHANGE
HOW WE LIVE, LEAD, AND LOVE

T.D. JAKES

WITH NICK CHILES

NASHVILLE   NEW YORK

Copyright © 2019 by TDJ Enterprises, LLP

Cover design by Kristen Paige Andrews
Cover photograph © Micah Kandros
Cover copyright © 2023 by Hachette Book Group, Inc.

FaithWords
Hachette Book Group
1290 Avenue of the Americas, New York, NY 10104
faithwords.com
twitter.com/faithwords

First edition: May 2023

FaithWords is a division of Hachette Book Group, Inc. The FaithWords name and logo are trademarks of Hachette Book Group, Inc.

The publisher is not responsible for websites (or their content) that are not owned by the publisher.

Bible verses are from the Holy Bible, New International Version®, NIV® Copyright © 1973, 1978, 1984, 2011 by Biblica, Inc.® Used by permission. All rights reserved worldwide.

The Hachette Speakers Bureau provides a wide range of authors for speaking events. To find out more, go to hachettespeakersbureau.com or email HachetteSpeakers@hbgusa.com.

FaithWords books may be purchased in bulk for business, educational, or promotional use. For information, please contact your local bookseller or the Hachette Book Group Special Markets Department at special.markets@hbgusa.com.

Interior book design by Timothy Shaner, NightandDayDesign.biz

ISBN: 9781546004011 (trade paperback)

Printed in the United States of America

LSC-C

Printing 2, 2023

CONTENTS

DISRUPTIVE THINKING

STUDY GUIDE

INTRODUCTION

Do you know the difference between hearing and listening? It's an important distinction.

Hearing is an auditory experience that involves noises. Sound waves pass into your auditory canal through your ears, which causes vibrations against your eardrum and the tiny bones of your inner ear. Those vibrations are amplified and transmogrified into the sensation we know as sound.

Hearing is a passive process that can be automated by your various membranes and neurons without your awareness. Indeed, if you remember back to the last time you sat next to someone who blabbered on about topics that didn't interest you in the slightest, you know it's possible to hear sounds without really processing them. That's why Jesus talked about people who "though hearing, they do not hear or understand" (Matthew 13:13).

Listening is different. Listening is a mental experience that involves thoughts. It's an active process that requires engagement. When I listen to someone, I not only hear the sounds they make, but I also focus on what they are saying. I consider the weight of their words. I ponder and respond.

I want to thank you for listening to what I have to say. That's what you are doing by participating in this study guide. There are powerful principles expressed in my book *Disruptive Thinking*. There are transformational truths tucked into those pages that have the potential to impact your life and your community in incredible ways. I know that from experience.

Therefore, I'm grateful you have chosen to engage those principles and those truths through the vehicle of this study guide. Doing so will give you the opportunity not only to dig deeply into what I've written, but to actively apply those words to your situation.

The material in this study guide is specifically designed to help you grapple with this critically creative skill I have labeled "disruptive thinking." We are living in a culture that is stagnating at a dangerous level. We need change agents. We need disrupters. We need you!

As you work through the material, you'll notice each of the six sessions is divided into two sections: one for personal study, and the other for group discussion. That first element is necessary because growth and development can be boosted by comprehension. Learning helpful information and skills allows us to change not just what we do, but *why* we do it.

The second element—group discussion—is also critical. Learning something new is only half the battle. You need to apply that knowledge in real-world situations in order to truly incorporate new information into your actions and attitudes. That kind of practice is greatly enhanced when you have the help and support of others.

The parameters of such a group are not defined. You may be part of a traditional small group or Sunday school class. You may host a book club at your home. You may gather each week with one or two friends to connect over important topics. You may have a mentor or spiritual parent who is guiding you through critical conversations.

All of these and more are valid expressions of transformational communities, and each is a valuable environment in which to explore the depths of *Disruptive Thinking.*

Go forth, then, and engage these concepts with enthusiasm! Be honest with yourself as you read and reflect. Be honest with others as you discuss and discourse.

And be ready to disrupt your world in ways that produce real and lasting change.

THE WHAT AND THE WHY

In this session, you will:

- Gain a better understanding of what it means to demonstrate disruptive thinking.

- Learn why disruptive thinking is necessary in today's world.

- Explore specific opportunities for disruptive thinking in your specific context.

- Join with others to review these themes and discuss how they apply to your lives and your community.

> Prior to engaging this session, read chapters 1 and 2 in the *Disruptive Thinking* book.

PERSONAL STUDY DAY 1:
WHAT IS DISRUPTIVE THINKING?

Most of us don't like to be disrupted.

We have our favorite spot on the sofa. Our favorite route for the daily commute. Our favorite flavor of coffee. Our favorite shows. Our favorite seats in church and our favorite booth at our favorite restaurant with our favorite waitress after the service.

Being knocked out of our comfort zone usually feels like a violation. Like an attack.

We prefer to be comfortable. We prefer to live in the known rather than risking the perilous possibilities that are always connected with new experiences and new ideas.

This is true on the level of individuals but also for society. That's why most of us make a habit of going with the flow, even if we don't realize it. When the cultural currents course strongly enough in a specific direction, we naturally drift in that direction as well. When everyone else says they like this new show or that new flavor, it's easiest to agree. (How else can we explain the preposterous proliferation of pumpkin spice every fall?) And when someone does something that upsets the apple cart in a major way, our first impulse is to frown. To shake our heads. *Who does she think she is?*

Is this bad? Is it a flaw in our DNA that we naturally seek out our own comfort? That we have a yen for zen?

I don't think so. Not always. Not entirely. Certainly it's true that we have a need as human beings for safety. Security. Stability. These are good gifts. They give us the ability to set down roots and grow.

But growth can turn into complacency, which is not good. Dullness is dangerous. Therefore, I believe there are seasons when we need a dose of what I call disruptive thinking—the ability to rise out of the comfortable currents of our snug beliefs and our contented bickering in order to blaze a new trail. To create something new. Something better.

In my opinion, we are currently living through one of those seasons.

What are some of your comfort zones? In what spaces or circumstances do you feel most comfortable?

_____

_____

_____

When was the last time one of those comfort zones was disrupted in a meaningful way? How did you respond?

_____

_____

_____

What does it mean to demonstrate disruptive thinking? There's no simple definition, but there are several characteristics we can explore together to gain a picture of what such thinking might look like in real life.

For starters, disruptive thinkers typically avoid the hot-button conflicts and conflagrations of the culture wars. Too many people waste too much time by arguing—they want so badly to be recognized as correct, to be part of the "right side," that they focus on the quarrel over all other considerations.

Not disruptive thinkers. They avoid arguments in order to seek solutions. They don't take sides; they take over.

Next, disrupters understand how to respond to trouble. That's in part because they understand that pain is not a feeling to be avoided but an opportunity to be exploited. Most people respond to difficulty by doing whatever they possibly can to return to normalcy, to regain their sense of safety and security. When something hurts, all we can think about is how to make the hurting stop.

Yet one of the keys to disruptive thinking is seeking out ways to thrive in the chaos—which usually means identifying the *new*. Creating new ways of doing things. Finding new possibilities. Blazing new trails when the old roads are all dead ends.

Disruptive thinkers choose to be unorthodox.

Chapter 1 of Disruptive Thinking *offers several examples of disruptive thinkers, including Elon Musk, Lena Horne, Abraham Lincoln, Jesus, and Mahalia Jackson. Which of those examples resonated most strongly with you? Why?*

_____

_____

_____

Take a moment to read through the major news headlines for today. Who are some possible disruptive thinkers making an impact in the world right now?

_____

_____

_____

In a general sense, how do you typically respond to pain or troubling circumstances?

_____

_____

_____

A final common characteristic of disruptive thinkers is their ability not only to handle criticism but to keep pushing forward in spite of detractors. Why is that necessary? Because people don't like to be disrupted!

For that reason, among many others, disruptive thinkers run the risk of becoming unpopular. And not just unpopular, but outright disliked. They have to deal with obstacles thrown in their path by people who assiduously stand for the status quo. Indeed, looking through the lens of history, disruptive thinkers are often unappreciated until long after they've been laid to rest in their graves.

I've experienced this reality in many ways. Consider these thoughts from the *Disruptive Thinking* book:

> But if you step off the beaten path, expect some thorns and briars. Initially it's quite natural to want to clear up any and all misperceptions about you. However, you have to eventually decide who you're trying to impact—your detractors or the world?
>
> You can't be a disruptive thinker while trying to negotiate peace settlements with people who want to define you by their description of you. Everyone who met me as a musician struggled to see me as a minister. Everyone who met me as a minister struggled to see me as an entrepreneur. Their snide remarks were born out of their discomfort with my mobility.

I couldn't afford to alter my definition of success to make my observers comfortable. Sooner or later a decision has to be reached that will set the tone for your lifelong priorities. Should you decide to be bold enough to be a drum major of a paradigm shift, you can't forever litigate the opinions of those who call fouls and plays from the bleachers. Whew! That took a while for me to learn. The sting of those you stun leaves deep welts. If you're not careful, you'll not fulfill your purpose in pursuit of their acceptance. Simply stated, are you willing to compromise your uniqueness for their camaraderie?

Standing up requires standing out.

When have you felt stung because you chose to stand out?

_____

_____

_____

How would you like to handle criticism? Meaning, what is your ideal way to respond to those who criticize you?

_____

_____

_____

PERSONAL STUDY DAY 2: WHY DO WE NEED DISRUPTIVE THINKING?

Now that we have a better understanding of what disruptive thinking looks and feels like, it's worth spending a few moments pondering its necessity. In short, why do we need disruptive thinkers in general, and why do we need them today? To begin, consider this excerpt from the *Disruptive Thinking* book:

> Why do we need disruptive thinking now? Ask that white rural man, who is staggered that his job prospects have disappeared, with no relief on the horizon. Ask that Black mother trying to figure out how to feed her family as her wages buy less with each passing month. Ask the worker gazing out the office window watching her CEO slide into the helicopter to ferry him to his private jet—as her health insurance coverage is slashed even further.
>
> Trust has been shredded. Anger is the new American pastime. If we are to be saved, we desperately need to summon the power of disruptive thinking.
>
> So, as we stand together on the precipice of the cliff, staring down into a valley teeming with unrelenting misery, we are all faced with the question for the ages: What are we going to do about it?
>
> What disruption are we willing to make in our lives to bring about change?

What emotions do you experience when you read the above quotation? Why?

_____

_____

Use the following assessments to evaluate your satisfaction with life over the past decade.

How satisfied did you feel with your life and experiences ten years ago?

1   2   3   4   5   6   7   8   9   10
(Totally unsatisfied)   *(Totally satisfied)*

How satisfied did you feel with your life and experiences five years ago?

1   2   3   4   5   6   7   8   9   10
(Totally unsatisfied)   *(Totally satisfied)*

How satisfied do you feel with your life today?

1   2   3   4   5   6   7   8   9   10
(Totally unsatisfied)   *(Totally satisfied)*

How would you answer that final question: What disruption(s) are you willing to make in your life to bring about change?

_____

_____

_____

Another reason we need disruptive thinking in the modern world is because the modern world has become a society of silos. As a people, we have been torn into tribes. Those who belong to this demographic are expected to think and act and vote and live a certain way—and only that way. Others who belong to that socioeconomic class carry the same expectations for conformity. Whatever "type" of person plays the largest role in your identity, that is the group to which you are irrevocably consigned.

You might think, *Hasn't it always been that way? Haven't Black people always been expected to coalesce around the same Black experience? Haven't rich people always been expected to say and do specific things? Haven't majorities always been expected to thrive and minorities always been sentenced to struggle?*

The answer to those questions is yes and no. Certainly those in specific demographic groups had a tendency to stick together in decades past. We naturally seek out those similar to us for safety and support. For help and healing. For community and correction.

But the rigid sectarianism of this moment is something new and something dangerous. Allegiances are demanded. Hatred is encouraged. And those who dare to question the wisdom of division are sentenced to the cultural chopping block through a system that features no judge and no jury—only executioners.

I firmly believe disruptive thinkers are required to bridge the gaps that are growing between groups today. We need those able to break down walls and reach across tribal divisions—those who can find common cause and create new pathways toward our common good. Our common future.

I'm committed to that mission. Are you? Are you brave enough to be a disruptive influence in your spheres of influence? In your community?

Because that's really the bottom line. The world isn't strained only on the edges of society. Things aren't bad just for other people. Your community is suffering, is it not? Your family, your friends, your coworkers—are they not angry? Are they not confused? Do they not despair for the future?

Yes, disruption is necessary in a world on the brink. The question for you and me is simple: What are we going to do about it?

What are some of the main sources of pain and dissatisfaction in your community?

_____

_____

_____

Take a moment to offer your answer to the question "Why is disruptive thinking necessary today?"

_____

_____

_____

PERSONAL STUDY DAY 3:
THE EXAMPLE OF JESUS

As we work through this study together, I will reserve one section of the personal study each week for the exploration of Scripture. Specifically, I want to take a deeper look at women and men in the Bible who operated as disrupters.

This week we'll start with Jesus. Because when you look through the Gospels, there's no doubt Jesus was a disruptive thinker par excellence.

There are many examples of Jesus demonstrating disruptive thinking, but I want to focus on a familiar story from the Gospel of Luke. To begin, read the following passage through twice. The second time, if you're able, read the verses out loud.

> On one occasion an expert in the law stood up to test Jesus. "Teacher," he asked, "what must I do to inherit eternal life?"
>
> "What is written in the Law?" he replied. "How do you read it?"
>
> He answered, "'Love the Lord your God with all your heart and with all your soul and with all your strength and with all your mind'; and, 'Love your neighbor as yourself.'"
>
> "You have answered correctly," Jesus replied. "Do this and you will live."
>
> But he wanted to justify himself, so he asked Jesus, "And who is my neighbor?"
>
> In reply Jesus said: "A man was going down from Jerusalem to Jericho, when he was attacked by robbers. They stripped him of his clothes, beat him and went away, leaving him half dead. A priest happened to be going down the same road, and when he saw the man, he passed by on the other side. So too, a Levite, when he came to the place and saw him, passed by on the other side. But a Samaritan, as

he traveled, came where the man was; and when he saw him, he took pity on him. He went to him and bandaged his wounds, pouring on oil and wine. Then he put the man on his own donkey, brought him to an inn and took care of him. The next day he took out two denarii and gave them to the innkeeper. 'Look after him,' he said, 'and when I return, I will reimburse you for any extra expense you may have.'

"Which of these three do you think was a neighbor to the man who fell into the hands of robbers?"

The expert in the law replied, "The one who had mercy on him."

Jesus told him, "Go and do likewise." (Luke 10:25–37)

Where do you see evidence of Jesus' disruptive thinking from this passage?

_____

_____

What principles did Jesus communicate here?

_____

_____

What can we learn about disruptive thinking through Jesus' methods of communication?

_____

_____

GROUP DISCUSSION

ICEBREAKER

Choose one of the following questions to begin your group's discussion for session 1.

- Who is an example in your life of someone who refuses to go with the flow?

  or

- When it comes to your daily choices—with your family, at work, in your neighborhood, and so on—are you more likely to create smooth sailing or to rock the boat? Explain.

CONTENT REVIEW

What ideas or principles did you find most interesting from chapters 1 and 2 of Disruptive Thinking?

What questions have been on your mind after reading those chapters? Or what seemed confusing that you'd like to have resolved?

There is no easy definition for what constitutes disruptive thinking. There is no template for how to go about the process of thinking in a disruptive way. But there are a few characteristics that disruptive thinkers seem to share in common. Here are three of those characteristics.

1. Disruptive thinkers avoid arguments and debates; instead, they focus their attention on identifying solutions.

2. They view trouble and painful circumstances as an opportunity to cut through the baloney and get important things done—all while advancing their own prospects in the process.

3. They don't allow themselves to be defined by critics or slowed down by opposition.

Work as a group to brainstorm a list of people from history who qualify as disruptive thinkers (for example, Abraham Lincoln). If possible, write that list on a whiteboard or large sheet of paper.

Next, have each person in the group vote for the two people on the list they believe to be the best examples of disrupters. Once the voting is finished, identify the three names with the highest number of votes.

What are some characteristics or traits those individuals share? What connects them?

How have those individuals impacted history? What are their most significant accomplishments?

Why do we need disruptive thinking in our world today? Because in so many ways, it feels like the deck is stacked so heavily against so many of us that humanity as a whole is losing hope. We've lost hope in our government. We've lost hope in the media. We've lost hope in the American dream. We've lost hope in the capitalist ethos of building a life worth living simply by working hard and living right.

The increasing absence of hope has been replaced by the addition of anger. We're all upset. We're all frustrated. We're all a bit bitter, and we all seem to firmly believe that all of our biggest problems are caused by the people we disagree with most. We've been told over and over that "the other side" is killing us.

For these reasons and more, I believe we've reached an inflection point as a culture. A tipping point. We need things to change in a major way, but nobody seems to know how to make those changes happen.

Well, here's the answer: We *make* them happen. We choose to change. You and me. We quit bickering about what isn't working, and we start figuring out what will work. We begin with our families, then our communities, then our tribes, then our nations, and then the world.

Where do you see evidence in today's world that people are losing hope in core institutions?

What are some of the main tribes or silos represented in your community? What are the different groups or cliques people stick to?

Where do you see opportunities to find common ground between those tribes and silos?

PRACTICE MAKES PERFECT

Take several minutes to practice disruptive thinking as a group by working together to modify a popular board game.

1. Identify a specific game that group members are familiar with—Monopoly, Uno, chess, Apples to Apples, and so on.

2. Work as a group to identify the major rules of that game, including what is required to win.

3. Brainstorm ways to disrupt those rules by coming up with a new way to play. Suggestions can be silly or serious, practical or impractical, grounded or farfetched. The goal is simply to practice the skill of not accepting "This is the way it's always been done." The goal is to practice disruptive thinking.

What are some of the major "rules" that govern our culture today?

When have you seen a person or an organization disrupt those rules successfully? What was the result?

WRAP UP

Remember these truths as you conclude this discussion for session 1:

- Disruptive thinkers avoid getting mired down in arguments, because they are seeking solutions.

- Disruptive thinkers see trouble and dissatisfaction as opportunities to implement real change.

- Disruptive thinkers choose to live with criticism rather than conforming to the expectations of others.

- We need disruptive thinking in today's world because we need to break loose from the tribes and silos that are increasingly dividing us and robbing us of hope.

MUTUAL DISRUPTION

In this session, you will:

- Learn why partnerships are a necessary element for maximizing the impact of disruptive thinking.

- Explore three keys for forming these partnerships: observation, communication, and integration.

- Discover what it takes to create collaborative solutions in today's world.

- Join with others to review these themes and discuss how they apply to your lives and your community.

> Prior to engaging this session, read chapters 3 and 4 in the *Disruptive Thinking* book.

PERSONAL STUDY DAY 1:
DISRUPTIVE PARTNERSHIPS

As you contemplate this concept of disruptive thinking, it's possible you are pondering a lone wolf type of arrangement. You may visualize disruptive thinkers as rogues who operate on the outskirts of society and constantly tell their would-be companions, "I work alone," like James Bond or Dirty Harry.

Let me dispel that fallacious fallacy by directly stating that nothing could be further from the truth. Disruptive thinkers are not isolated individuals who make a singular impact. Instead, they form meaningful partnerships that allow them to maximize the reach and the breadth of their disruptive ideas.

Even the examples I mentioned above are flawed. James Bond is an agent of MI6, which means he's part of a huge network of spies and supplemental personnel. He's got M to cast the vision and Q to equip him with the latest gizmos and gadgets. Ditto for Dirty Harry, who is part of a sprawling police force with sprawling resources.

My point is this: disruptive thinkers are team players. They may not "work well with others" by their intrinsic nature, but they understand the necessity of cruising with a crew—of squaring up as part of a squad.

Therefore, a core component of disruptive thinking is the ability to recognize your own limitations. You must understand not only what you do well but also where your weaknesses lie. And you must have the ability to create meaningful partnerships with others who can amplify those strengths and taper those weaknesses.

Such an approach does not need to be complicated. Indeed, many of us have already done the groundwork of creating disruptive partnerships in our key relationships: husband and wife, parent and child, employer and employee.

Critically, the most functional and successful partnerships are often those that avoid homogeneity. Meaning, if I partner only with people who look, think, and behave like me, then there is little extra benefit to those collaborations. But when I create connections with those who are different from me—those who have different skills, different worldviews, different audiences, and more—then I dramatically expand the reach of what I can achieve.

Use the space below to write down three of your longest and healthiest relationships. This can include family, friendships, business arrangements, and more. Next to each name, write down several words that describe the relationship in question.

1._____ : _____

2._____ : _____

3._____ : _____

In general, are you more effective or ineffective when it comes to building healthy partnerships? Explain your answer.

_____

_____

_____

What is required in order to form meaningful disruptive partnerships? Three skills are paramount: observation, communication, and integration. Let's explore each of those a little more deeply together.

First, in any situation where a new partnership is formed—whether voluntarily or through some other means—observation is essential. There is much that needs to be figured out in order for that partnership to thrive, and we start that process by observing. By staying attuned to every detail and every situation.

What are we watching for? A primary goal is watching how your partner contributes to this relationship—what they offer and how they offer it. What benefits do they contribute? Similarly, what rewards or outcomes are they expecting? What do they hope to gain? What constitutes a "win" or a healthy relationship for them?

Too many partnerships are ruined because both parties operate out of their own strengths and goals, rather than assessing the strengths and goals of their partner. Such an assessment requires observation.

Next, developing a disruptive partnership requires communication. In fact, observation and communication *must* be paired together. If you observe what you need and what your partner needs, yet you don't communicate those observations or ask important questions, you will both be operating in the dark. If you communicate without first making observations, you'll be prone to many wrongheaded conclusions.

Observation and communication work in tandem. No one steps into a new situation already possessing the knowledge necessary to thrive. We must observe. Similarly, none of us can observe so effectively that we can make decisions and blaze pathways in such a way that benefits all involved, our partners included. We must communicate in order to succeed.

Look back at the three important relationships you recorded above. What have you observed about your partner in each of those relationships? What makes them tick? What are their strengths? Weaknesses?

1._____ : _____

2._____ : _____

3._____ : _____

In general, what are some challenges that hinder your ability to communicate effectively?

_____

_____

_____

Once you have employed observation and communication, the final step is *integration*—learning how to use the information you've obtained from observation and communication. It's the critical step of integrating that information into your actions and decisions. What you *do*.

That's key. In order to help bring about the transformation our culture desperately needs, you need to be not only a disruptive thinker but also a disruptive doer. You need to find partners who can help you change information into action.

We'll explore that step in more detail in day 2 of this personal study section.

PERSONAL STUDY DAY 2:
COLLABORATIVE SOLUTIONS

It's been my observation that some people confuse "disruptive thinking" with "disordered thinking" or even "disturbing thinking." They believe a disrupter is someone who charges in like a bull in a china shop, just tearing down whatever they can reach and demanding change.

That won't work. The bull (or the idealogue with a megaphone) rarely accomplishes anything helpful—and certainly not on purpose.

Instead, as we highlighted in previous pages, true disruptive thinkers take the necessary time to assess the situation before taking action. They observe. They communicate. Then, once they possess the requisite information, they spring into action.

That action is what I refer to as "integration"—taking the information we've gained through observation and communication and using it in a manner that effects change. Not just change, but positive change. Transformation.

Here is an example from the *Disruptive Thinking* book of what integration looks like (and could look like) in my community:

> Many institutions like ours are a trusted voice in the community. No, not everyone trusts any institution anymore. But no one sees as many people of color on a weekly basis as houses of faith. The influence of the church in the Black community continues to rise, according to recent Barna Group research reports. Also, the church building itself is the most underutilized, highly expensive resource on the ledger of fiduciary responsibility in most communities—affording us the ability to host STEM programs, daycare for struggling mothers, food banks, and reentry programs—all accomplished through foundations and community development corporations.

Disruptive thinking asks, "How can we better utilize our facilities, staff, and influence to bridge the gap between services, suppliers, and recipients?" This question led to the development of the T.D. Jakes Foundation. I wanted to be sure that the missionary work we were doing in the community had its own identity and could exist between the community and the church more effectively. Many of the services that the foundation provides were already being done by the church, but were not sustainable merely by tithes and offerings. In fact, if you took all the income from all of the churches in the United States and put it up against the budget that is needed for welfare, healthcare, eye care, transportation, groceries, utilities, rental assistance, and surgeries, it is obvious you would run out of resources within sixty days. So, the notion that we could do it alone was a fantasy. Here's a disruptive thought for you: maybe churches could be connective tissue between government agencies, corporations, and community leaders and collectively do it together.

Where do you see examples of observation in the paragraphs quoted above?

_____

_____

Where do you see opportunities for communication?

_____

_____

Take a moment to dream big about the type of integration suggested in those paragraphs. What might it look like in your community if the church stepped up to serve as a bridge between people in need and those with the resources to meet those needs?

_____

_____

_____

Let me emphasize once more that the kind of transformative solutions we are all seeking will require collaboration. Not just an individual seeking to make a little change here and a little change there, but mutual disruption. Collaborative partnerships.

And in order for such partnerships to become fruitful, we must be willing to look beyond ourselves and those who by every metric are the same as ourselves. We must be willing to find common ground with the "others" of our community. The acquaintances. Those who hang their hats on the other side of the tracks. Even those we have considered antagonists in the past.

Consider your backyard. (If you don't have a backyard, imagine one for your future.) Could you improve your backyard by planting one type of seed?

Yes. If you used all of your available space to plant lettuce seeds, you could grow an abundance of lettuce. Doing so would provide a source of food—lettuce for your salads. Fresh lettuce to garnish your burgers and sandwiches. Then more lettuce for more salads. Growing lots of lettuce could also improve your air quality by providing more plant life to work as natural filters. There would be benefits for sure of layering yourself in lettuce.

But think of the same yard growing many different kinds of plants. Could you produce more improvement simply by diversifying what you reap and sow?

Again, the answer is a clear yes. With just a little foresight, you could produce a garden bursting with flavors. Lettuce and carrots and cucumbers and green beans and peppers and potatoes and kale and radishes. What else? There are so many options, and I'm getting hungry just thinking about them! Not just flavors, though—think of the colors. Think of green and red and orange and yellow and purple. Think of the textures as you walk through that garden and run your fingers across a panoply of leaves and stalks and flowers.

Let's not make this more complicated than necessary. One person thinking disruptively can make a difference. That's absolutely true. Many similar people working together can make a bigger difference—a bigger impact. But in terms of true disruption and true results, the best possible outcome is to create a team of people with different ideas and different backgrounds and different skills, all working together to change the world.

What are some ways you currently interact with and engage people who are different from you?

_____

_____

_____

Where do you see spaces in your community where people of different stripes and different types can come together and connect in meaningful ways?

_____

_____

_____

PERSONAL STUDY DAY 3:
RAZING THE ROOF

What does it look like to see a collaborative partnership in action? We can get a good glimpse in this important story from the Gospel of Mark. As you read, pay attention not only to Jesus and the man He healed, but also to the team that opened up the door for this transformational moment.

Read the following scripture twice, then answer the questions that follow.

> A few days later, when Jesus again entered Capernaum, the people heard that he had come home. They gathered in such large numbers that there was no room left, not even outside the door, and he preached the word to them. Some men came, bringing to him a paralyzed man, carried by four of them. Since they could not get him to Jesus because of the crowd, they made an opening in the roof above Jesus by digging through it and then lowered the mat the man was lying on. When Jesus saw their faith, he said to the paralyzed man, "Son, your sins are forgiven."
>
> Now some teachers of the law were sitting there, thinking to themselves, "Why does this fellow talk like that? He's blaspheming! Who can forgive sins but God alone?"
>
> Immediately Jesus knew in his spirit that this was what they were thinking in their hearts, and he said to them, "Why are you thinking these things? Which is easier: to say to this paralyzed man, 'Your sins are forgiven,' or to say, 'Get up, take your mat and walk'? But I want you to know that the Son of Man has authority on earth to forgive sins." So he said to the man, "I tell you, get up, take your mat and go home."

He got up, took his mat and walked out in full view of them all. This amazed everyone and they praised God, saying, "We have never seen anything like this!" (Mark 2:1–12)

Here are the protagonists of this story. What strengths or abilities did each person or group bring to the table in that moment?

Jesus: _____

The paralyzed man: _____

The four friends: _____

Where do you see examples of collaboration and partnership within this story? (Think of all that apply, including verses 8–12.)

_____

_____

_____

What are some dreams or hopes you have for your community that would cause people to say "We have never seen anything like this"?

_____

_____

_____

GROUP DISCUSSION

ICEBREAKER

Choose one of the following questions to begin your group's discussion for session 2.

- What's the best team you've ever been part of? How did you add to that team?

  or

- On a scale of 1 (terrible) to 10 (terrific), how well do you typically "play with others"?

CONTENT REVIEW

What ideas or principles did you find most interesting from chapters 3 and 4 of Disruptive Thinking?

What questions have been on your mind after reading those chapters? Or what seemed confusing that you'd like to have resolved?

Now that we've explored the what and why of disruptive thinking, this session is focused more on the how. Namely, how do we leverage disruptive thinking in a way that produces results?

The first answer is that disruptive thinkers are most effective when they don't try to go it alone but instead form meaningful partnerships that produce powerful results. True disrupters are not renegades who march to their own beat and answer to no one. Instead, they are team players who are able to maximize their own strengths and skills by harnessing additional strengths and skills from others.

Remember this truth from the *Disruptive Thinking* book: "There is nothing worse than being disruptive and being alone. Not only is it emotionally challenging, but we are likely to be less effective. We are most productive when we have a whole community of people who galvanize around that disruption and support it."

When have you tried to make a change or accomplish something on your own? What happened?

What are some skills, experiences, or resources that would have been helpful in achieving your goals?

Two necessary skills for demonstrating disruptive thinking within a partnership or team environment are observation and communication.

Observation assumes you don't have all the answers. Rather than ramming through your plans without regard for the ramifications, first take some time to observe the environment in which you find yourself. Observe the conflict or issue you are trying to improve. What caused it? What are some possible ways to solve it? Also observe your partner(s) in your collaborative environment. What are their strengths and resources? What are their goals? What do they need from you now?

Once you've done some observing, the next step is communication. Talk about the information you've gained. Work with your partner(s) to learn what they need from you. Be clear and upfront about your goals, your intentions, and how you plan to measure success or failure.

These two critical tools—observation and communication—will open a plethora of doors for any collaborative exercise and dramatically increase your overall chances of success.

Think of a partnership you've observed that works really well—two spouses, a business relationship, a deep friendship, etc. Where do you see observation and communication evident in that partnership?

After observation and communication comes a third characteristics of disruptive collaborations: integration. This is the act of transformation information into action. Because ultimately disruptive thinking will be unhelpful if it does not transition to disruptive doing.

One way to prevent stagnation and inaction is to intentionally expose yourself to different types of people. Consider these truths from the *Disruptive Thinking* book:

> Think a moment about reproduction. It is the story of opposites—when men and women get together, their differences complement each other, and their fruit becomes evidenced through the birthing of new life. The child is a product of their unity and their uniqueness. The cross-pollination among flowers, carried by bees, adds to the harvest time of the fruit of the trees. No one sits down to eat a meal that has no diversity on the plate. Everything around us is demanding that we get out of our comfort zones, our silos, step away from our comrades, and join the broader stream of society in order to provoke lasting change.
>
> I have learned over the years that when all your associates are in your same field, do what you do, and know what you know, the only thing that can be born from the association is repetition, competition, or envy. I challenge you to get out of your comfort zone and into circles and spheres of influence that are built around what you do not do and do not duplicate what you already have accomplished. This man in the Bible surrounded himself with people who did not have the same weaknesses as he did. Consequently, he was able to be lifted, carried, and transported to a positive solution.

Work as a group to evaluate the latent power you possess as a group. What strengths are represented in this room?

What are some potential obstacles that could hinder you from working as a group to accomplish something bigger than the sum of your parts?

PRACTICE MAKES PERFECT

Spend the next five minutes discussing a hot-button issue that is currently affecting your community. This could be education, housing, demographics, food shortages, and so on. Pick something that is bound to create some conversation.

Here's the caveat: have two or three volunteers sit on the edge of the group and observe rather than talk. These observers are charged with learning whatever they can about their fellow group members, about the dynamics in the group, and about the topic under discussion—but they can only operate through observation.

When five minutes have passed, allow the observers to share some of their more interesting observations. If time allows, repeat the process with a new set of observers.

What did you learn about yourself through this exercise?

What did you learn about your group?

WRAP UP

Remember these truths as you conclude this discussion for session 2:

- Trying to be a disruptive thinker on your own is frustrating and typically ineffective. Partnerships are required to produce real change.
- Successful partnerships move forward through observation, communication, and integration.

- It's critical that you not limit yourself to collaborating exclusively with others who are similar to yourself. Variety will create opportunity and success.

- Sooner or later, disruptive thinking will need to become disruptive action in order to achieve any real transformation.

COUNTING THE COST

In this session, you will:

- Be reminded of the sacrifices that must be made in order to think and live disruptively.
- Examine service as the true motivation for disruptive thinking.
- Explore what it takes to jump the invisible fences that were built, intentionally or unintentionally, to keep us in line.
- Join with others to review these themes and discuss how they apply to your life and your community.

> Prior to engaging this session, read chapters 5 and 6 in the *Disruptive Thinking* book.

PERSONAL STUDY DAY 1:
WHY DISRUPT?

Much of what we've covered so far in this study guide has been preparatory. We've explored what disruptive thinking is and why it's necessary in a broad sense. We've dispelled the myth that disruptive thinkers are lone wolves, and we've lifted up the value of collaboration in implementing disruptive solutions.

Now I need to offer a warning: disruptive thinking doesn't come cheap. There is a price to be paid—often many prices, or a single price that needs to be paid over and over and over again. For that reason, the life of a disrupter isn't something to adopt casually. Don't think disruptively on a whim. As Mordo warned in the first Doctor Strange movie, "The bill comes due."

Consider these comments from the *Disruptive Thinking* book:

> Success doesn't feel successful. That may sound counter-intuitive, almost like an oxymoron, but hear me out. The biggest misconception people have about reaching what they would consider "success" is what it will feel like when they get there. We work our behinds off, toiling away in the dark of night, putting pleasure and family time on hold, all with the goal of getting to that magical place we have dreamed about. But when we get there, we quickly discover it's not the fantasy we had created in our heads. We find out there are all sorts of accoutrements—wanted and unwanted—that go along with success. There's a lot of pain, which steals away the savory satiety that we thought would greet us there. Success doesn't feel successful; it feels hard. It's not necessarily going to make us happy. It can be lonely. A lot of the sacrifices we made along the way come home to roost, with repercussions popping up in unexpected places, biting us in the behind.

The key word in those paragraphs is *sacrifices*. Disruptive thinking always includes a tuition. It requires us to pay a price.

The problem comes when we make those sacrifices in pursuit of a feeling. For many people, success is the feeling of elation that comes after a goal is achieved. It's the jubilation of announcing that promotion or posting pictures of that ring or cashing that check. But feelings fade. They don't last. And when the feeling is gone, we are left to wonder whether the price we paid was worth something so temporary.

Instead of getting caught in the trap of chasing feelings, take some time right now to create a concrete picture of what success will mean for you.

Use the space below to draw a picture of what successful disruptive living might look like in this phase of your life. You could draw a diploma, for example, or something that represents the impact you desire to have in your community. Be concrete. (If you're not an artist, remember that representing something visually forces you to think in a new way, so do your best and give it a try.)

Next, use the space below to flesh out your vision of success. What will it mean for you to effectively disrupt your life or your community in a way that creates a positive impact? Be as specific as you can.

_____

_____

What are some sacrifices that will be necessary in order to bring that vision to reality?

_____

_____

Maybe you're wondering, *Why should I pay the price to think disruptively? Why should I make that sacrifice?* The answer is because you want to change the world. You want to make an impact in your community. You want your life to *matter.*

Me too.

What we need to understand is that true success always involves more than just you and me. It's about making a positive impact in the lives of others. It's about effecting real and lasting change in a world that is broke and getting broker every day.

The truest form of disruptive thinking involves not just sacrifice, but service.

Jesus washing His disciples' feet is one of the most striking moments in the Gospels. Take a look for yourself to see what I mean:

> The evening meal was in progress, and the devil had already
> prompted Judas, the son of Simon Iscariot, to betray Jesus.
> Jesus knew that the Father had put all things under his
> power, and that he had come from God and was returning

to God; so he got up from the meal, took off his outer cloth-
ing, and wrapped a towel around his waist. After that, he
poured water into a basin and began to wash his disciples'
feet, drying them with the towel that was wrapped around
him. (John 13:2–5)

Talk about disruptive thinking! The Savior of the world stripped not only
of divinity, but now of dignity. The hands that fashioned galaxies dipped into
a bucket of dirty water to wash the dirt and debris from His disciples' dusty,
crusty, calloused feet.

In that moment, Jesus gave us a picture to follow, an example to live. True
leadership is a service to humanity—not to ourselves. It's not about being allot-
ted and applauded; it's about leveraging your influence to provoke some change,
or to protect, or to prepare. That is the essence of disruptive thinking.

So let me ask you: whose feet have you washed in pursuit of genuine,
world-changing success?

*When have you been in a position to truly serve someone—to "wash
their feet"? What did you experience in that moment?*

_____

_____

*Look again at your picture of success recorded above. How will that
picture serve others in ways that create positive change?*

_____

_____

PERSONAL STUDY DAY 2:
WHY IT'S SO DIFFICULT

Let's talk for a moment about fences.

As you know, fences are everywhere in our world. They separate house from house. Neighborhood from neighborhood. Even nation from nation. Most people think of a fence as something designed to keep people out of a place. But most often what fences accomplish is keeping people penned in.

That's true about the physical fences we see all over the place, but it's also true about the internal fences each of us is carrying in our minds and hearts—what I often refer to as invisible fences. Here's how I describe that phenomenon in the *Disruptive Thinking* book:

> The reality is that we all have invisible fences in our lives, quietly working to hold us back, to make us afraid, to curtail our attempts at boldness. To stop us from being disruptive. In chapter 2 I talked about the time when I screamed at the TV set because I saw a young man say he was trapped in his neighborhood. I said that he could escape his circumstances—he could be poor anywhere in America, even on the beach. My response was logical, but what I failed to do was to recognize his invisible fence. There was something keeping him in that community that I couldn't see from my comfortable couch.
>
> When you were growing up, did someone tell you that you were stupid, or ugly, or goofy, or awkward? Or that you were shy or lazy? Or your nose is too wide? Or your ears are too big? Have those words established a permanent home in your psyche, where they have been living rent-free for twenty or thirty years or more, chipping away at your self-esteem, making you timid and uncertain? The fears and insecurities

that we carry around with us are invisible fences, carefully constructed and reinforced by the negativity of others, woven together to form an intimidating barbed-wire barrier that continues to imprison us.

These invisible fences often explain why we sometimes fail to act in ways that would benefit us most. How often have you wondered, *Why do I keep doing this? Why do I keep getting stuck in this problem?* The answer often comes down to the invisible boundaries that bind up our thinking and box us in.

For that reason, we can't think and act as disrupters until we've identified the invisible fences that are holding us in place. Use the following questions to help consider your own personal cages.

When you were growing up, what made your parents (or guardians) pleased? How did you earn their approval?

_____

_____

_____

What are some of the significant labels people have placed on you throughout your life? (Examples may include smart or dumb, attractive or ugly, hardworking or lazy, rich or poor, popular or unpopular, and so on.)

_____

_____

_____

What were you deprived of in your growing-up years? What resource or blessing was consistently lacking in your home?

_____

_____

_____

Once you identify a fence that has been hemming you in, it's easy to make it seem like you've jumped it. It's easy to give that impression. That's why people buy luxury cars and park them in front of dilapidated homes. It's why folks can walk around with the latest Jordans on their feet but no retirement in the bank. They are putting on a show.

This is where disruptive thinking moves us forward. Because disruptive thinking isn't just about breaking rules and shaking things up. No, disruptive thinking is all about sustainability.

When we get to the other side of the fence, we need a plan to live there successfully. We need to have a sense of how to live and grow; otherwise, we'll feel uncomfortable and jump back into the life we've always known.

So, once you've identified one of the fences that has been holding you back, it's time to put on your thinking cap. What steps will be required to tear that fence down? What will it look like to move beyond the limits in which you lived previously? What resources will be required to find success on the other side?

Incidentally, this is another reason why collaboration is so critical for disruptive thinking, because you can't always answer these questions on your own. Having someone who isn't bound up by your own internal borders is a great boon for moving forward.

What's an example of an invisible fence that has limited your mobility in life?

_____

_____

_____

What might your life look like if that fence was torn down? How would things be different?

_____

_____

_____

PERSONAL STUDY DAY 3: REMOVING FENCES

There are many examples of women and men in Scripture who were forced to deal with invisible fences. I think of all the younger sons who were told by their culture that they were not as valuable as their elder brothers: Jacob, Joseph, David, and more. I think of Ruth, who was an outsider by race and by gender, yet overcome those cages to take her place in the genealogy of Christ.

But the most striking story of invisible fences has to be Gideon. Read the following passage twice to get a better sense of what I mean.

> The angel of the Lord came and sat down under the oak in Ophrah that belonged to Joash the Abiezrite, where his son Gideon was threshing wheat in a winepress to keep it from the Midianites. When the angel of the Lord appeared to Gideon, he said, "The Lord is with you, mighty warrior."
>
> "Pardon me, my lord," Gideon replied, "but if the Lord is with us, why has all this happened to us? Where are all his wonders that our ancestors told us about when they said, 'Did not the Lord bring us up out of Egypt?' But now the Lord has abandoned us and given us into the hand of Midian."
>
> The Lord turned to him and said, "Go in the strength you have and save Israel out of Midian's hand. Am I not sending you?"
>
> "Pardon me, my lord," Gideon replied, "but how can I save Israel? My clan is the weakest in Manasseh, and I am the least in my family."
>
> The Lord answered, "I will be with you, and you will strike down all the Midianites, leaving none alive."
>
> Gideon replied, "If now I have found favor in your eyes, give me a sign that it is really you talking to me. Please do

not go away until I come back and bring my offering and set it before you."

And the Lord said, "I will wait until you return."

Gideon went inside, prepared a young goat, and from an ephah of flour he made bread without yeast. Putting the meat in a basket and its broth in a pot, he brought them out and offered them to him under the oak.

The angel of God said to him, "Take the meat and the unleavened bread, place them on this rock, and pour out the broth." And Gideon did so. Then the angel of the Lord touched the meat and the unleavened bread with the tip of the staff that was in his hand. Fire flared from the rock, consuming the meat and the bread. And the angel of the Lord disappeared. When Gideon realized that it was the angel of the Lord, he exclaimed, "Alas, Sovereign Lord! I have seen the angel of the Lord face to face!"

But the Lord said to him, "Peace! Do not be afraid. You are not going to die."

So Gideon built an altar to the Lord there and called it The Lord Is Peace. To this day it stands in Ophrah of the Abiezrites. (Judges 6:11–24)

What were some of the visible fences or obstacles that had limited Gideon's mobility in life?

_____

_____

_____

What are some of the invisible fences that had hemmed in Gideon prior to the angel's arrival? Circle the evidence of those fences in the text above.

_____

_____

_____

Skim through the rest of Gideon's story in Judges 6–8. How did God guide Gideon through the process of tearing those fences down?

_____

_____

_____

GROUP DISCUSSION

ICEBREAKER

Choose one of the following questions to begin your group's discussion for session 3.

- What images come to mind when you think about "the other side of the fence"?

  or

- When have you done a poor job of counting the cost before starting a project or making a big decision? What happened next?

CONTENT REVIEW

What ideas or principles did you find most interesting from chapters 5 and 6 of Disruptive Thinking?

What questions have been on your mind after reading those chapters? Or what seemed confusing that you'd like to have resolved?

Strange as it sounds, success can cause a short-circuit in our ability to demonstrate disruptive thinking. Many would-be disrupters begin the march toward change with honest motives and the desire to move mountains. But when they reach a pinnacle in their journey, they freeze. Afraid of losing what's been gained, they stop moving forward and become a monument rather than a movement.

Other times success causes us to focus on ourselves more than is helpful. When we begin to see our efforts produce fruit, we are in danger of thinking too highly of ourselves—or of thinking of ourselves too often. We forget that true leadership is an offering to others and instead create an idol of our own accomplishments.

The best way to prevent success from becoming an obstacle is to stay focused on service. When we can wash the feet of others, as Jesus did, we will be following His example of creating lasting change in a broken world.

When has someone self-sacrificially served you in a way that made a meaningful impact on your life?

Speaking generally, what are some obstacles that prevent us from making more of an effort to serve those in need throughout our community?

We spent a lot of time considering fences in the personal study material for this session. There are invisible fences that have been erected in our minds and hearts as individuals. These fences often determine what we believe possible or appropriate without us being aware of their influence in our lives. They hem us in and hold us down.

The same is true of our communities and even our countries. So many of us are boxed in by boundaries established long before we were born.

Therefore, a vital step in the process of disruptive thinking is taking the time necessary to step back and identify those fences. What assumptions are we carrying? What limits have we placed on ourselves, and what limits were assigned to us by others? What do we believe we cannot accomplish?

What did you learn about yourself as you considered your own invisible fences during the personal study portion of this session?

When have you seen someone successfully remove one of the invisible fences present in their mind or heart? What happened next?

As you continue to gain an understanding of what disruptive thinking is and how to incorporate it in your life, let me again advise you to count the cost.

Because yes, there will be a cost to living as a disrupter. I believe that cost is worth it, but you'll need to evaluate the transaction for yourself.

Why does your community need disruptive thinkers? What's at stake if you and your group allow things to remain as they are?

PRACTICE MAKES PERFECT

To start this exercise, divide into subgroups of between two and four people each. Then, work through the following scenario and answer the questions in italics. Before concluding the gathering, come back together as a group and compare notes and plans for this exercise.

Here's the scenario: your group has been selected to receive $1 million from a billionaire benefactor to make a positive impact in your community. You will receive that money in one lump sum, and then it will be up to you to determine how to spend it in a way that produces actual change.

What will you do? Use the following questions/prompts to guide your discussion.

What is the core problem you would like to address and eventually solve?

What are specific positive outcomes you want to see? What are the solutions you want that $1 million to buy?

How will you structure your solution? Will it be a business? A nonprofit? A one-time donation? Something else?

How will you address the sustainability issue? What can you do to structure your solution so that it lasts for years? Even decades?

WRAP UP

Remember these truths as you conclude this discussion for session 3:

- A key step for learning how to think disruptively is identifying the fences (visible or invisible) that are hemming you in.

- Fences can be removed or bypassed in numerous ways, but it always takes effort on our part. Nobody is going to do that work for you.

- Remember that disruptive thinking comes with a cost. Count that cost for yourself and your family before you move forward.

- If we're not careful, success can become a challenge we need to overcome in order to achieve meaningful change in our world.

CONFRONTING CHALLENGES

In this session, you will:

- Review some of the major obstacles that will present themselves when you jump the fence as a disruptive thinker.

- Learn key methods and principles for overcoming those obstacles.

- Learn how to address the core question of disruptive thinking: *Why?*

- Join with others to review these themes and discuss how they apply to your lives and your community.

> Prior to engaging this session, read chapters 7 and 8 in the *Disruptive Thinking* book.

PERSONAL STUDY DAY 1:
MAJOR OBSTACLES ON THE WAY TO DISRUPTION

I mentioned earlier that being uncomfortable is a consequence of disruptive think-ing. They call them "comfort zones" for a reason, and when we intentionally jump the fence to leave the known and reach the unknown, we're going to expe-rience discomfort. Disquiet. All manner of disturbances.

One of the aspects of that discomfort that surprises many would-be disrupters is our own ego. By that I mean the way we see ourselves. The picture we carry in our minds of who we are and how we relate to the world around us.

Are you a big fish in a small pond? That's a good feeling. You're known. You're valued. You're trusted and appreciated. But choosing to think and act disruptively will likely require you to lose that location and surrender that status.

Jumping the fence usually means becoming a small fish in a huge pond—even an ocean. At least for a little while.

On a practical level, that means you will become exposed to people who are smarter than you. Stronger than you. Better liked than you. More successful than you. More creative than you. More connected than you. And yes, wealth-ier than you.

Actually, jumping the fence requires you not only to be exposed to the big fish in the big pond, but also to *intentionally seek them out.* You need to search for those who are living out your dream, and you need to sit at their feet. Humbly. Quietly. You need to listen and learn.

That can be tough on anybody's ego. Which is why so many would-be disrupters end up going back to their little pond. Because being small again—even for a little while—is too much to bear. Your ego is an obstacle to your dreams of disruption.

How do you see yourself in your community right now? What are
some of the main factors or characteristics that define who you are?

_____

_____

_____

When was the last time you remember your ego being bruised? How
did you respond?

_____

_____

_____

Disruptive thinking is dangerous not only to your ego, but also to the egos of others. When you engage your community as a disrupter, you will force others to deal with their own comfort zones—you may even push them out into uncharted waters.

They won't like it. They'll come at you with guns blazing.

For that reason, disruptive thinkers need to know how to overcome obstacles such as criticism, condemnation, and even personal attack. This is especially true in a culture that values cancellation far above conciliation.

The first key to overcoming those obstacles is to understand that criticism is not a crisis. It's not a failure. It's not a sign that something is wrong. Instead, criticism is often an indicator that you're on the right track. Why? Because comfortable people don't condemn what keeps them comfortable. They only get riled up when they've been riled up. Criticism is evidence of disruptive thinking.

Next, how you handle that criticism will go a long way in determining your level of success. True disruptive thinkers know that legitimate critiques offer a chance for legitimate improvement. You don't have all the answers—not right away. As you begin the process of disruptive living, you are going to make some mistakes. Criticism is an opportunity to identify those mistakes and then move beyond them.

How can we use criticism as a springboard for improvement? By asking one simple question: *Is it true?* When people come to you with their denigrations and denunciations, listen to what they are saying. Take a step back and evaluate. *Is there any truth to this? Is any part of this criticism accurate? Are my critics highlighting a genuine gaffe or opportunity for growth?*

If the answer to those questions is yes, then you've got some work to do. But you've also got a great chance to grow.

If the answer to those questions is no, then you are free to ignore the shots coming your way. It is important that you don't engage with those shots. Don't get argued into an argument. Don't become cornered in a quagmire. The old saying is true: "Never wrestle with a pig, because you'll both get dirty—and the pig likes it."

What are some criticisms you've received in the past year? Take a moment to think, and then write down everything that comes to mind. Include critiques at work and at home. Include shots against your performance and personality.

_____

_____

Now the hard part. Which of those criticisms are true? Use the space below to write down critiques that hit the mark. Then, write down possibilities for improvement in those areas.

_____

_____

PERSONAL STUDY DAY 2:
THE CHALLENGE OF SUCCEEDING

One of the reasons disruptive thinking is difficult is because it always involves change—and change is difficult. Most people don't like to change and don't want to change. That includes disrupters. It also includes the people who are disrupted by our disrupted thinking. Our families, for example. Our neighbors. Our coworkers.

For that reason, being successful as a disruptive thinker will create a whole new level of challenges. That includes a lot of criticism, as we've already discussed. Disrupters need to be comfortable with discomfort.

But success itself can become a challenge for those who think disruptively. When you start to see real change in your life and in the community around you, you'll have to deal with the consequences of that change.

For instance, you might have to carry the weight of expectation on your shoulders. People often expect you to repeat your success over and over again. If your success is financial, that will open up a whole new can of worms. Money is both a blessing and a responsibility. Success brings you in contact with new people and new circumstances, both of which may also include new perils.

And through it all, you will need to deal with the urge to settle for the success you've achieved rather than maintaining your drive to keep going, keep pushing, keep changing.

Think back to some of the ways your life has changed over the past five years. In what ways has your situation improved?

_____

_____

_____

When has a blessing resulted in unexpected challenges in your life?

_____

_____

_____

How can we maintain our edge and our passion as disruptive thinkers even through the crucible of success? By focusing on our core.

Lifting weights is a key discipline for many who strive for the goal of physical fitness. Yet sometimes a personal trainer will shake things up by introducing a large, somewhat soft, somewhat bouncy ball into the equation. Instead of leaning back against a stable bench to perform a chest press, for example, the trainer will require you to drape yourself over the ball as you attempt to lift the weight.

Why? Because the instability of the ball forces you to engage the muscles in your core—your back, abs, obliques, and glutes. No matter how much you can curl with your beach-worthy biceps, you will not be a healthy specimen if your core is feeble.

Carrying that metaphor forward, a key step in becoming a disruptive thinker is to address what we might call the core of your life. This core can be summarized in one small-yet-stimulating word: *Why?*

Why are you doing what you are currently doing? Why are you working at your specific job? Why are your relationships in their present state? Why are you unable to kick certain bad habits or pick up certain good ones?

Disruptive thinking starts by asking, "Why are things the way they are?" And the first place that question needs to be aimed is yourself.

Consider these thoughts from *Disruptive Thinking* on the necessity of strengthening your core:

> The only way to survive in this environment is to not worry about what the world says. You must define your own center

and know who you are as a person—not what you got, not what you own, not what you wear, not what they demand of you. Who are you right here and now? Because if you're going to jump, if you're going to speak, if you're going to take on this assignment or evolve into this new element or bring somebody into your life, you must have a sense of who you are as you're trying to learn the new assignment. This is a moment to strengthen your core—your why. That means understanding why you're jumping in the first place and what it means to you. Is this something you really want to do—or something you're trying to do because your sister did? Or because the only way your father validates you is when you respond in certain ways? Or because Instagram is telling you that this is something you should be doing?

Take a moment to address your core—your why—in connection with these major categories of life.

Why are you working at your current job? What are the reasons that brought you there and keep you there?

_____

_____

Why are your closest relationships your closest relationships? What causes you to invest time and energy in those connections?

_____

_____

Why do you tolerate specific harmful habits or patterns of behavior in your life?

_____

_____

_____

As I say, the "Why?" question is the core of disruptive thinking. It is our first step in the process of learning to think disruptively—first about your own situations, and then about the broader world around us.

So, take a moment to apply the "Why?" question to the broader world around you. Specifically, your own community.

What is an issue that continues to be a problem for your community, something people want to solve but have never solved?

_____

_____

_____

What are some of the whys connected to that issue?

_____

_____

_____

Why did it begin? What caused it?

_____

_____

_____

Why does it bother people? Why is it a problem?

_____

_____

_____

Why hasn't it been addressed or fixed? What are the obstacles that have prevented a solution?

_____

_____

_____

PERSONAL STUDY DAY 3: UNDIGNIFIED LEADERSHIP

Earlier I mentioned ego as an obstacle to the kind of disruptive thinking that leads to transformation and success. Jumping over our familiar fences can cause us to be confronted by our smallness relative to others. Such confrontations are unpleasant, but often necessary.

As I read through Scripture, I'm startled by the number of people who had to be stripped of their ego before they could be useful members of God's kingdom. Think of Jacob eating his just deserts from Laban's underhanded hand. Think of Moses moving from luxury in Pharaoh's household to lack in the wilderness. Think of Paul preaching for three years in Arabian obscurity before finally connecting with the church leaders in Jerusalem.

Think also of David. As a seventh son in a world where birth order was critical, David learned humility at an early age. And, unlike many, he was able to maintain his humble spirit even when he reached the top.

Here's an example of what I mean. Read the following Scripture passage two times, then answer the questions that follow.

> Now King David was told, "The Lord has blessed the household of Obed-Edom and everything he has, because of the ark of God." So David went to bring up the ark of God from the house of Obed-Edom to the City of David with rejoicing. When those who were carrying the ark of the Lord had taken six steps, he sacrificed a bull and a fattened calf. Wearing a linen ephod, David was dancing before the Lord with all his might, while he and all Israel were bringing up the ark of the Lord with shouts and the sound of trumpets.
>
> As the ark of the Lord was entering the City of David, Michal daughter of Saul watched from a window. And when

she saw King David leaping and dancing before the Lord, she despised him in her heart.

They brought the ark of the Lord and set it in its place inside the tent that David had pitched for it, and David sacrificed burnt offerings and fellowship offerings before the Lord. After he had finished sacrificing the burnt offerings and fellowship offerings, he blessed the people in the name of the Lord Almighty. Then he gave a loaf of bread, a cake of dates and a cake of raisins to each person in the whole crowd of Israelites, both men and women. And all the people went to their homes.

When David returned home to bless his household, Michal daughter of Saul came out to meet him and said, "How the king of Israel has distinguished himself today, going around half-naked in full view of the slave girls of his servants as any vulgar fellow would!"

David said to Michal, "It was before the Lord, who chose me rather than your father or anyone from his house when he appointed me ruler over the Lord's people Israel—I will celebrate before the Lord. I will become even more undignified than this, and I will be humiliated in my own eyes. But by these slave girls you spoke of, I will be held in honor." (2 Samuel 6:12–22)

What are some ways David demonstrated effective leadership in this passage?

_____

_____

_____

Based on this passage, what are some specific ways David created a positive impact in his community? How did he serve others?

_____

_____

_____

Where do you currently have an opportunity to let go of your dignity in order to honor God and others?

_____

_____

_____

GROUP DISCUSSION

ICEBREAKER

Choose one of the following questions to begin your group's discussion for session 4.

- When have you overcome an obstacle in a way that made you feel proud?

  or

- What emotions do you typically experience when you are challenged by another person or a difficult circumstance?

CONTENT REVIEW

What ideas or principles did you find most interesting from chapters 7 and 8 of Disruptive Thinking?

What questions have been on your mind after reading those chapters? Or what seemed confusing that you'd like to have resolved?

There are a few things in this world that are both meaningful to experience and easy to achieve. Holding your spouse's hand, for example, or laughing with your child until both of you have watery eyes and tender tummies. Those joyful memories are ripe for the plucking whenever we are wise enough to see them.

Most of the time, however, truly meaningful achievements require a truly terrific amount of effort. They require hard work and sacrifice. And they typically necessitate overcoming quite a few obstacles in the process.

That is certainly the case with disruptive thinking. In order to push for real and lasting change in our communities, we will need to push through challenges of many kinds.

One such challenge is our own ability to adapt in new situations. Leaving your comfort zone by definition means becoming uncomfortable. Will your ego allow you to become smaller in your own eyes before you grow into a better version of yourself? Will you have the energy to keep up with new competitors and achieve new goals? These are critical questions.

Speaking of critical, criticism is another challenge on the road to disruptive thinking. The more you seek to create positive change, the more you will disrupt those who are content with current circumstances—and the more you will be criticized. How you respond to that criticism will go a long way toward determining whether you can transform disruptive thinking into disruptive living.

Who in your life does a good job of handling criticism?

When have you been thrown into a new situation that required you to adapt? How did you respond?

Every parent remembers the "Why?" phase of their child's development. During those months, it seems you can't go two minutes without hearing a little voice asking a large question.

"Why do we go to bed at night?"

"Why is that flower red?"

"Where does the moon go during the day?"

"Why?" digs at the heart of a matter. It is an exploratory question, demanding answers. It is a question that assumes solutions are not only possible, but can be found right around the corner.

"Why?" is also the foundational question for disruptive thinking. It is the critical query that helps us better understand who we are, what motivates us, and what will be required to move us from where we are to where we want to go.

Focus the "Why?" question on yourself for a moment. What are some of the core desires or goals that motivate you to do what you do?

Now focus that question on our culture as a whole. What are some of the main motivators that drive people in our society?

PRACTICE MAKES PERFECT

In chapter 5 of the *Disruptive Thinking* book, I highlighted five important resources each of us needs to be willing to lay aside in order to serve others. Those are:

1. *Time.* This is such a precious commodity; putting it aside speaks volumes.

2. *Title.* This means coming in the form of a servant, not a master. Dropping your PhD and serving beans and potato salad with the rest of us. Not hiding behind your massive accomplishments, your Oscar, your own version of an Oscar—whatever you're extremely proud of. Can you risk laying that aside?

3. *Talent.* Okay, you might be able to run the whole agency, but are you willing to mentor, expose people to creative influence, give your talent away to the dreams and aspirations of more than self-aggrandizement?

4. *Treasure.* Yes, this one is about money. No investment means no return. It's going to cost something to do anything truly impactful.

5. *Temperament.* Are you willing to risk managing your emotions differently to make yourself available for people that don't normally fit the profile of the people you like to be around? Possessing the emotional maturity to manage moods, opinions, and preferences of personality types for the greater good is essential. People who don't can't grow with you.

In the previous session of this study guide, you created a picture of what disruptive thinking and disruptive living might look like in this phase of your life. Use that picture or idea as the foundation for discussing the five questions below within your group. (If helpful, divide into smaller groups of three or four people each.)

What does it look like for you to set aside your time in order to serve others? How does that currently happen?

What are some titles or accomplishments you tend to display or hide behind? What does it mean for you to lay those aside when necessary?

Which of your specific talents can be applied to your picture of disrupting your community in a positive way?

When have you invested financially in yourself in a way that felt like a sacrifice? What would it look like to make a similar investment in others?

What aspects of your temperament (personality or character) might make it difficult to serve others in your community? What can you do to lay those aspects aside?

WRAP UP

Remember these truths as you conclude this discussion for session 4:

- Ego can be a major obstacle that prevents us from thinking and living disruptively.
- Disruptive thinking will produce discomfort. We can count on it.

- Disruptive thinking will also bring about criticism and condemnation—even personal attacks. The way we handle that criticism will go a long way toward determining our level of success.

- The core question for disruptive thinkers is "Why?" That is where we start.

SUPPORTING A DISRUPTER

In this session, you will:

- Consider how to support disrupters in a business setting.
- Consider how to support disrupters in a classroom setting.
- Consider how to support disrupters within a close relationship.
- Join with others to review these themes and discuss how they apply to your lives and your community.

Prior to engaging this session, read chapters 9 and 10 in the *Disruptive Thinking* book.

PERSONAL STUDY DAY 1:
MANAGING OR TEACHING A DISRUPTER

Every person has the ability to demonstrate disruptive thinking. I believe that strongly, which is why I have written these materials. Disruptive thinking is a skill that can be learned; it is a pattern of thought and action that can be adopted by anyone to create change in specific situations.

That being said, not every person is a disrupter. In fact, most people are not. Disrupters are those to whom disruptive thinking is as natural as breathing. They can't help thinking disruptively; it's how they are wired.

I am a disrupter. I have encountered many other disrupters during my decades of working in business, music, ministry, and film. But I have also realized that true disrupters—those who can't help but live disruptively—are relatively few and far between. That's probably a good thing; otherwise, we would live in a state of constant distraction or destruction.

My point is this: chances are good you are not a disrupter yourself. Perhaps you've already come to that conclusion as you've worked your way through this material. If so, let me say again that is okay! You have been designed for a purpose, and you can benefit from the ability to think disruptively when doing so is helpful.

Still, chances are also good that you will encounter disrupters many times in your life. Perhaps at work. Perhaps in the classroom. Perhaps in your neighborhood. And perhaps even in your own bed, if you are married to a disrupter. Therefore, let's spend some time in this session exploring what it looks like to support, guide, and encourage a disrupter in those venues.

*Based on what you've encountered in this study, do you consider
yourself a disrupter? Explain.*

_____

_____

_____

*Who are some true disrupters you have encountered over the course
of your life? How did you respond to those encounters?*

_____

_____

_____

One of the greatest desires all people possess is the desire to be seen, to be
recognized and valued not for what we can contribute to others but for who we
are. Each of us has a need to be truly known and appreciated.

This need is especially critical for disrupters in our world today. Why? Because
too often disrupters are viewed as difficult. Problematic. Even antagonistic. When
a disrupter makes waves in your classroom or your company, it's easy to focus on
those waves rather than the person involved. It's easy to label them as problem
causers or troublemakers rather than potential agents of change.

One of the best things you can do to support a disrupter in your sphere of
influence is take the time to truly see them. Recognize their value. Speak openly
about their worth and their potential for positive change.

In other words, see them. Let them know: *I see you.*

But that doesn't mean you automatically bend to a disrupter's will and give
them free rein. As I wrote in the *Disruptive Thinking* book:

Since we are talking about disruptive thinkers, leaders need to know that in some of these scenarios the disrupter may be a change agent who is trying to push us to change the way we operate. They might walk into the building wanting to shake things up, insinuating that the way things were done before doesn't work for them, or that they have ideas about how to do it better. The leader should try to get them to back up a bit. In order to be effective, disrupters must employ a sense of diplomacy that respects the culture that predates them—but have the fortitude to offer ideas to potentially disrupt that culture. Also, the submission to understand that not every idea will be accepted, not every idea may be right for the company. Not every idea is a good idea. That requires some humility. When it comes to growth and development in organizations, there isn't just one right answer. The disrupter's idea might not work in the current market, or at that particular time of the year. Disrupters must engage in a delicate dance in organizations. If the boss doesn't let their idea win the day, it may trigger feelings of rejection, which could prompt the disrupter to flee. Everybody has to be sensitive and aware of how quickly the relationship can sour.

Think again about the disrupters you have encountered in recent years. Were they known more for who they were or for the disruption they caused?

_____

_____

_____

Consider one or two disrupters currently operating in your sphere of influence. What steps can you take to see them in a significant way?

_____

_____

_____

In addition to recognizing the value of disrupters in our different venues, the next step we can take in supporting their important work is to create environments in which that work can be accomplished safely and effectively. Meaning, we have to create environments that allow for potential disruption. This is true all the way from a kindergarten classroom to the executive boardroom.

How do we create such an environment? First, by choosing to stay flexible. The way things were done before doesn't always work now—it *shouldn't* always work now. Change is necessary, which is why disrupters are necessary. Choose to focus on the people rather than the waves. Be willing to adapt.

Second, the best way to manage disrupters in every setting is to keep the lines of communication wide open. Listen to them. Talk with them. Understand what they are saying and *why* they are saying it. That doesn't mean you must always agree with them or that their ideas should always be implemented.

But teach them rather than punish them. Speak with them rather than ignore them. Offer them guidance and support.

This is especially important in our educational system today—and especially difficult. As I wrote in the *Disruptive Thinking* book:

> In many ways, the challenge schoolteachers face is figuring out a way to level up the classroom when students from a vast array of circumstances walk through the door. Some kids will have eaten a full breakfast and been driven to school, while another might have left a house without break-

fast after watching their mother get beaten half to death the night before. One kid hasn't seen their mother in months and is living with an overwhelmed and destitute grandmother, while another doesn't even have a home to live in. Those kids clearly are not going to be in the same position to learn and thrive, yet that's the school system's expectation. They will be compared to one another every day and penalized if they don't perform in a way that far-off education bureaucrats have deemed they should. And, increasingly, the teachers also will be penalized if their students don't meet state standards. It's a brutal, disturbing system.

If they are able to make it to college, the kids from chaotic homes and underfunded schools will be expected to perform at the same level as kids from well-to-do homes with stable families. For those kids, the floors have never been flat and the rules continue to be unclear.

When have you been part of an environment where disruptive thinking was allowed or even encouraged?

_____

_____

Reread the paragraphs above regarding our educational system today. Where do you see possibilities for improving that system in your community?

_____

_____

PERSONAL STUDY DAY 2:
BEING MARRIED TO A DISRUPTER

Marriage is difficult under any circumstance. It requires hard work. It requires sacrifice. It requires patience and love and the ability to communicate. Why? Because people are unique. Marriage is the combination of two distinct and distinctly different individuals into a single, functional organism. Such an amalgamation will always be extremely difficult to achieve.

Even so, marriage is completely, totally worth it. The opportunity to know and be known by someone in the deepest form of intimacy is one of the greatest gifts we can receive as human beings.

I know all this from experience. Likely you do as well.

So, let me depart from the typical structure of these sessions by offering several key principles that can be helpful to remember (and practice) in any deep relationship where disruption is part of the experience.

Stop fighting to be right. It's a constant temptation in any relationship to deal with conflict by assigning yourself as the "correct" party and the other person as "incorrect." Marital issues can rarely be boiled down to right and wrong, black and white, guilty and innocent. True change comes when we stop fighting to prove our correctness and start investing that energy into finding solutions.

Your lover is not your enemy. When you experience conflict or disturbance within a relationship, it is critical to separate the issue from the individual. The easiest thing you can do in the midst of a disagreement is to try to best the person with whom you disagree. The most productive thing you can do is join forces with that person in order to tackle the root issues at the heart of that disagreement.

Trust is about more than fidelity. Broken trust is a poison for any relationship. But it's important to remember that trust can be severed in ways other than sexual infidelity. Trust plays a huge role in our finances, for example, and emotional connection, and much else. Therefore, it's helpful to make a distinction between actions and motivations as we navigate the waters of marriage.

Understanding doesn't necessarily align with condoning. Empathy is the ability to understand what another person is feeling or experiencing, and then supporting that person out of *their* unique perspective rather than your own. Meaning, it's possible to understand what someone is going through without condoning those experiences. This ability to empathize and support others through traumas and disappointments is critical in marriage.

Agree to disagree. My final principle is perhaps the most important within the context of disrupters. Simply stated, it's okay to disagree. Even on big things. Even on core issues. Disagreement with your disrupter does not require dissolution of your union. You can say, "This is my opinion, and that is your opinion, so let's drop this subject and go do something else."

Use the following scales to evaluate your closest relationships as disrupters.

To what degree is your spouse a disrupter?

1   2   3   4   5   6   7   8   9   10
(In no way)   *(In every way)*

To what degree is your best friend a disrupter?

1   2   3   4   5   6   7   8   9   10
(In no way)   *(In every way)*

To what degree is your boss a disrupter?

1   2   3   4   5   6   7   8   9   10
(In no way)   *(In every way)*

To what degree are your parents disrupters? (Make a circle for your mother and a square for your father.)

1   2   3   4   5   6   7   8   9   10

(In no way)   *(In every way)*

What are some of the main sources of conflict you experience with disrupters?

_____

_____

_____

Which of the principles described above feels most important in your current relationships? Why?

_____

_____

_____

Based on what you've learned about disrupters in this study, what are some ways to avoid viewing them as the enemy?

_____

_____

_____

To what degree are you able to agree to disagree with those closest to you? How can you grow in that skill?

_____

_____

_____

PERSONAL STUDY DAY 3:
A SUPPORTIVE ENCOURAGER

There are many famous marriages in the Bible. Abraham and Sarah. Jacob and Rachel. Ruth and Boaz. David and Bathsheba. Priscilla and Aquila. Yet in this section I want to discuss a marriage that wasn't a marriage—not technically. It was a ministry partnership that, as you'll see in the passages below, generated a wonderful amount of fruit for God's kingdom.

I am talking about Paul (also known as Saul) and Barnabas.

In many ways, those two men were as different as could be. Paul was a disrupter par excellence. He constantly pushed, constantly challenged, and constantly ground his way forward for the sake of the gospel. Barnabas, on the other hand, was more comfortable behind the scenes. He was a supportive encourager. Together, they changed the world.

Read these Scripture passages through two times, then answer the questions that follow.

> When he came to Jerusalem, [Saul] tried to join the disciples, but they were all afraid of him, not believing that he really was a disciple. But Barnabas took him and brought him to the apostles. He told them how Saul on his journey had seen the Lord and that the Lord had spoken to him, and how in Damascus he had preached fearlessly in the name of Jesus. So Saul stayed with them and moved about freely in Jerusalem, speaking boldly in the name of the Lord. He talked and debated with the Hellenistic Jews, but they tried to kill him. When the believers learned of this, they took him down to Caesarea and sent him off to Tarsus.
>
> Then the church throughout Judea, Galilee and Samaria enjoyed a time of peace and was strengthened. Living in

the fear of the Lord and encouraged by the Holy Spirit, it increased in numbers. (Acts 9:26–31)

Now those who had been scattered by the persecution that broke out when Stephen was killed traveled as far as Phoenicia, Cyprus and Antioch, spreading the word only among Jews. Some of them, however, men from Cyprus and Cyrene, went to Antioch and began to speak to Greeks also, telling them the good news about the Lord Jesus.[21] The Lord's hand was with them, and a great number of people believed and turned to the Lord.

News of this reached the church in Jerusalem, and they sent Barnabas to Antioch. When he arrived and saw what the grace of God had done, he was glad and encouraged them all to remain true to the Lord with all their hearts. He was a good man, full of the Holy Spirit and faith, and a great number of people were brought to the Lord.

Then Barnabas went to Tarsus to look for Saul, and when he found him, he brought him to Antioch. So for a whole year Barnabas and Saul met with the church and taught great numbers of people. The disciples were called Christians first at Antioch. (Acts 11:19–26)

Where do you see evidence that Paul was a disrupter in his world?

_____

_____

_____

What are some specific ways Barnabas created a safe environment for Paul to demonstrate disruptive thinking?

_____

_____

_____

Read Acts 15:36–41, which describes a sharp disagreement between Paul and Barnabas. What can we learn from those verses about handling conflict in close relationships?

_____

_____

_____

GROUP DISCUSSION

ICEBREAKER

Choose one of the following questions to begin your group's discussion for session 5.

- What's one big lesson you've learned about relationships over the course of your life?

  or

- When has a teacher or mentor made a big difference in your life?

CONTENT REVIEW

What ideas or principles did you find most interesting from chapters 9 and 10 of Disruptive Thinking?

What questions have been on your mind after reading those chapters? Or what seemed confusing that you'd like to have resolved?

Being in a relationship with a disrupter is often a disruptive experience. That goes for many types of relationships—in school, at work, at home, and beyond. Disrupters are designed by their Creator to disrupt things, which can make non-disrupters feel uncomfortable. Even unsafe.

Still, being close to a disrupter does not have to be a source of pain. In fact, it's often a blessing when we navigate those relationships in the right way.

For example, most disrupters are used to being unseen. They've often been told something is wrong with them at the core—that they just keep causing problems. When you take the time to know and value these individuals, you meet their needs in a way that helps them feel validated in their own skin. You tell them it's okay to be who they are, which is an incredible gift.

Next, when you find yourself in contact with a disrupter, it's important to offer a safe environment in which they can operate. Don't assume everything should continue to operate in the way it has always operated. Instead, allow disrupters to share their ideas and offer their insights. Even if you don't adopt the plans they suggest, you will be rewarded, because disrupters see the world from a different angle than most other people. You'll have the benefit of another point of view.

Ultimately, your goal is to help disrupters lead the way in disruptive thinking without creating a situation that is destructive. That requires a lot of communication.

In your own words, how would you describe what it looks like to create a safe environment in which disrupters can operate?

What are some steps we can take to engage with disrupters in a way that does not cause us to feel bullied or overrun?

Remember why we've been talking about these topics for the past five sessions: because disrupters are important! They have a critical role to play in our culture and in our world.

As I wrote in the *Disruptive Thinking* book:

> Nobody writes about rule followers. They're not the ones who turn heads and transform systems. But if you're still afraid of leaping over that fence, just consider that the thinking we now consider orthodox used to be seen as disruptive. Imagine the eye-bulging consternation that greeted the first dude who decided to hunt for edible mushrooms that wouldn't kill you. Or the first person to conclude that it was okay to drink the milk from a cow or a goat. The new orthodoxy used to be disruptive. What is now widely accepted at some point was looked upon as heresy. This should be solace to

the ears of all the disrupters out there—if you're right, they all will soon be following you.

But if you're a true disrupter, that will be your signal to find the next fence to leap over.

In what specific ways have you benefited from disruptive thinking?

In specific ways have you benefited from having disrupters in your sphere of influence?

PRACTICE MAKES PERFECT

It's time for some role play. If your spouse is part of your group, partner with them. Otherwise, find a partner and choose the role you will play together— spouse, boss, best friend, coworker, and so on.

Once you've determined your roles, take turns working through the following scenarios. In each scenario, one of you will be the disrupter, and the other will be attempting to support, guide, or encourage the disrupter within that situation.

Here are the scenarios (remember to take turns acting as the disrupter):

- The disrupter is a business owner who wants to borrow a large amount of capital in order to take the business to the next level. The disrupter has a plan for how to spend the money and what they expect those expenditures to achieve, but the partner is not convinced the return will be worth the risk.

- The disrupter is a spouse who wants the family to relocate to a new state in order to pursue new business opportunities. This is not the first time the disrupter has had such an idea or impulse—there have been many in the past—and the partner wants to gauge how serious the disrupter is about what would be a major shift for the family.

- The disrupter is a low-level marketing manager in a medium-sized company who wants to revamp the way that company approaches marketing. The disrupter is convinced the current marketing strategy, which was developed ten years ago, is out of touch with new technology and new audiences. The disrupter has a plan to approach the CEO with the new ideas, but the partner wonders if it's better to work within the system rather than jumping over people's heads.

WRAP UP

Remember these truths as you conclude this discussion for session 5:

- The key to managing and supporting disrupters is creating an environment in which they are safe being themselves.

- The goal for disrupters should be to initiate disruption without destruction.

- Many systems in our culture put disrupters at a disadvantage, including our educational system.

- Being married to a disrupter can be a big blessing and a big challenge, often at the same time. The secret to making it work is to celebrate each spouse's uniqueness and communicate through the differences.

KEEP MOVING FORWARD

In this session, you will:

- Explore the aspects of raising children who are inherently disruptive.

- Consider how to encourage and support a child who is also a disrupter.

- Highlight the need to keep moving in our journey toward success—to keep pressing forward.

- Join with others to review these themes and discuss how they apply to your lives and your community.

Prior to engaging this session, read chapters 11 and 12 in the *Disruptive Thinking* book.

PERSONAL STUDY DAY 1:
PARENTING A DISRUPTER

In the previous session, we explored the unique challenges and opportunities that come with stewarding relationships with disrupters in several key areas of life—at work, in the boardroom, in the classroom, in the bedroom, and more. What's important in those situations is helping to create an environment in which disrupters are safe to be themselves and do the work they were created to do, yet not become destructive. It's an important balance.

In this final session of our study together, I want to spend some time focusing on the unique phenomenon of parenting a disruptive thinker.

To start, we need to understand that the nature of children is inherently disruptive. When we plant a seed in soil, nobody is surprised when that seed sprouts and disrupts the earth around it, bursting upward in new strength and new life. Yet how often are we surprised—and even aggravated—by the disruptions in our world caused by the generations that come behind us?

Here's what I wrote in the *Disruptive Thinking* book:

> The great thing about every new generation is they are predisposed to test the boundaries. That's what young people do—they push past the guardrails and try to set their own course. In other words, they feed off disruption, looking for new and hopefully better ways. Because we have a fidelity to a system that fit our era, sometimes we misunderstand their disruption as rebellion, not recognizing that time has made our old parameters almost irrelevant. Children are taught by previous generations—whether by parents or teachers—who have a dogma and a creed that is built around their experiences, which are often not applicable to the situations the children find themselves in today.

What are some words you would use to describe your childhood?

_____

_____

_____

How did your family respond when you or someone else rocked the boat in your home?

_____

_____

_____

One of the simplest traps we can slip into as parents is to prefer it when our children are "easy," when they think like we do, act like we prefer them to act, and fit well into the system—in our home, in the neighborhood, at school, and beyond. Kids who make waves make work for Mom and Dad, and it's common for parents to resent that work.

This becomes an issue with disrupters because they are almost never "easy." They don't adapt to the systems already in place. Instead, disrupters typically demand that the system change to accommodate *them*. The cruel irony of our homes and our classrooms is that we ask our children to sit still and listen quietly to stories about heroes from history who refused to sit still and listen quietly— heroes who refused to fit in.

Let me offer two quick principles for parenting a disruptive thinker. First, parents must go beyond teaching and spend time listening in order to figure out who their children are. Each child is a unique individual, just like you are unique. They have unique genes and unique dreams. The only way to understand what they are is through conversation and through listening.

Second, once you've listened and have a good understanding of who your child is, do everything you can to place them in the right environment for them to grow. Plant them in a situation in which they can flourish.

For disruptive thinkers, that means placing them in a space where they are able to think disruptively without being shut down or shut out. It means having a home that is flexible enough to ride the waves and even to endure seasons of trials and trouble. Such seasons are often the crucibles in which disrupters are formed.

Think about your culture and community. What are some of the systems in which children are expected to fit in without making waves?

_____

_____

_____

In what situations does your child open up and share about who they are?

_____

_____

_____

Let me offer a final thought on this subject. In many cases today, children who think disruptively are not only labeled as defective but diagnosed as such in a medical sense. As I wrote in the *Disruptive Thinking* book:

When we are faced with a disruptive child, before we bring in the heavy artillery of psychiatrists and psychologists and drugs like Ritalin, before we make the child feel like they have a sickness, we must make sure the problems can't be resolved by more focused parenting. We live in a world where we want to respond to every "problem" with a quick fix. An estimated one out of every thirteen children in the US takes some sort of psychiatric medication. But with parenting, you don't fix anything quickly. The fastest way to get there is slowly. Of course, there are some children who need medical assistance to cause their brains to function effectively. But pills have become a catch-all solution for busy people to resolve every child's problems. In the US, we medicate our children far more than any other country. In many cases, there may be other factors at work, other reasons they are acting up that don't require drugs to fix.

The work of parenting is difficult. Always. That's true whether you have a child who sometimes thinks disruptively or a child who is a natural disrupter. That's true if you have one child or one dozen. The work is hard.

Yet the rewards are great. So keep working. Keep listening. Keep planting. And keep trusting.

PERSONAL STUDY DAY 2:
RAISING THE SAVIOR

I made the case in previous pages that all parenting is hard work, largely because all children are inherently disruptive. Now I want to take a moment to prove those assertions through Scripture by looking at a moment in Jesus' childhood.

As a parent to five children and a grandpa to nine, I have seen my share of disruption in the family setting. I've helped raise my share of disrupters—which is only fitting, since I grew up as a disrupter myself. But I can't imagine what it must have been like to parent someone as disruptive as the Creator of the universe and the Savior of the world bundled up in the bubbling, exuberant body of a child.

To see what I mean, read this Scripture passage two times, then answer the questions that follow.

> Every year Jesus' parents went to Jerusalem for the Festival of the Passover. When he was twelve years old, they went up to the festival, according to the custom. After the festival was over, while his parents were returning home, the boy Jesus stayed behind in Jerusalem, but they were unaware of it. Thinking he was in their company, they traveled on for a day. Then they began looking for him among their relatives and friends. When they did not find him, they went back to Jerusalem to look for him. After three days they found him in the temple courts, sitting among the teachers, listening to them and asking them questions. Everyone who heard him was amazed at his understanding and his answers. When his parents saw him, they were astonished. His mother said to him, "Son, why have you treated us like this? Your father and I have been anxiously searching for you."

"Why were you searching for me?" he asked. "Didn't you know I had to be in my Father's house?" But they did not understand what he was saying to them.

Then he went down to Nazareth with them and was obedient to them. But his mother treasured all these things in her heart. And Jesus grew in wisdom and stature, and in favor with God and man. (Luke 2:41–52)

What can we learn from these verses about Jesus' character—about who He is?

_____

_____

_____

_____

How do these verses foreshadow Jesus' role as a disrupter in His community? In history?

_____

_____

_____

_____

Look again at verse 50: "But they did not understand what he was saying to them." Growing up, what did you feel like your parents or guardians did not understand about you?

_____

_____

_____

_____

What specific steps can you take to seek out a greater understanding of the children currently in your life?

_____

_____

_____

_____

PERSONAL STUDY DAY 3:
WHAT WE MUST DO NOW

As we approach the end of this study guide, let's take a moment to review the ground we covered.

For starters, disruptive thinking is exactly what it sounds like: the kind of thinking and living that disrupts the status quo. It's an explosive form of creativity that refuses to settle for what's already there and instead focuses on what could be—on what *will* be. Disruptive thinkers are agents of change. They are often the catalysts that push cultures and communities into the future.

We need such thinkers today. Why? Because when we look around at the current iteration of our culture, we see silos everywhere. Bunkers. Cliques. The whole world feels like an argument, and everyone is taking sides—everyone except disrupters. Instead of taking sides, they take control. That needs to happen today.

As we've seen, disruptive thinkers are not lone wolves or rogue operators. They are not independent of the systems around them. The best disrupters—those who actually make an impact in their own lives and in their communities—are those who understand the power of partnership. Of collaboration.

On their own, disrupters are typically irritating. Leading a team, however, they are irresistible. Such teams are the driving force behind the collaborative solutions we desperately need in modern society.

Of course, like most things that matter, disruptive thinking does not come easily. Neither does the kind of disruptive living that produces positive change. There are obstacles that need to be overcome. Many of those obstacles are personal and internal: our ego, our ability to adapt, and our response to the taste of success. Many challenges are external: systems and individuals will resist change by criticizing and ostracizing those who don't fit their preferences.

One key to overcoming these challenges is to ensure that disrupters have a safe environment in which to be themselves. They require space to ask questions and push boundaries. This is true in the classroom, the boardroom, and the bedroom. For that reason, the best way to manage a relationship with a disrupter is communication. Talk with them rather than simply reacting to them. Learn who they are and what they need.

What are some of the most important concepts you have uncovered in this study? What makes them important to you?

_____

_____

_____

Having come to the end of this study guide, how would you rate your ability to think disruptively when you want to?

1   2   3   4   5   6   7   8   9   10
(Nonexistent)   *(Flourishing)*

Let's break it down even further: How would you assess your ability to think disruptively in the following areas of life?

At home (your family)

1   2   3   4   5   6   7   8   9   10
(Nonexistent)   *(Flourishing)*

At work (your career)

1   2   3   4   5   6   7   8   9   10
(Nonexistent)   *(Flourishing)*

At church (your spiritual life)

1	2	3	4	5	6	7	8	9	10

(Nonexistent)   *(Flourishing)*

Personally (in your own mind)

1	2	3	4	5	6	7	8	9	10

(Nonexistent)   *(Flourishing)*

What's next? Now that you've worked your way through this deep dive on the subject of disruptive thinking, what is the next step forward?

I don't know the answer for you specifically. But I know what you must do is keep stepping. Keep moving forward. As I wrote in the *Disruptive Thinking* book:

> Whether you just discovered yourself from stealing tennis shoes, whether you are stuck in the middle of the jarring leap over the wall—with pain so intense that you're wondering whether it was even worth it to leap—or whether you've landed on the other side of something that is so unfamiliar that you don't even know what to call it, *keep moving.* You may have worked yourself into a room for which you have no point of reference, no experience to understand. You may be sitting in a place that looks magical, that feels transcendent, but is almost too good to believe. *Is this truly me?* you may be asking yourself, as you fight off impostor syndrome. Regardless, *keep moving.*
>
> If you stay there long enough, foreigners become citizens. Immigrants become leaders. We're all immigrants during the first stage of crossing over the fence. But if you work hard enough, if you own it, if you don't run away from it, even-

tually the system will embrace you. You will become one of them. You will belong.

If you must, reach out for help along the way. Cry if you feel it's necessary. Don't be afraid. A friend once told me this: Tenacity will get you there. Consistency will keep you there. Gratefulness will give you more of what's there.

Keep moving.

Where do you have an opportunity to demonstrate disruptive thinking in your personal life this week?

_____

_____

_____

Where do you have an opportunity this week to think disruptively at work? What might that look like?

_____

_____

_____

What are some obstacles that have prevented you from disruptive thinking in the past?

_____

_____

_____

What is one step you can take this week to "jump the fence" for one of those obstacles?

_____

_____

_____

GROUP DISCUSSION

ICEBREAKER

Choose one of the following questions to begin your group's discussion for session 6.

- What is one important thing you have learned about parenting over the course of your life?

  or

- What's one of your favorite things about your family right now?

CONTENT REVIEW

What ideas or principles did you find most interesting from chapters 11 and 12 of Disruptive Thinking?

What questions have been on your mind after reading those chapters? Or what seemed confusing that you'd like to have resolved?

It's a story that's been told a thousand times and more. A child grows up in a family environment that feels solidified. The goals and values have been ossified over time. Four generations of doctors, and now it's your turn to get in line for the MCAT. Or your father and your grandfather didn't need college to succeed in life, so why would you? We didn't raise you to waste your time on that kind of nonsense.

Families are filled with systems, boundaries, and expectations. And when those limits are pushed or transgressed by a child, the simple solution is to label the child as the problem. "She doesn't fit in." "He needs to learn how to fall in line."

These conflicts and conflagrations happen with all types of children, but they are especially common when a disrupter is in the home, because those who think disruptively will automatically question the fish bowl in which they were born. Oftentimes they'll be driven by an urge to see just how far the boundaries can be pushed.

For these reasons and more, parenting a disrupter requires patience and a commitment to communication. Instead of always asking the "Why?" question of our children—"Why did you do that?" "Why can't you do it this way?" "Why are you like this?"—we should consider asking the "Who?" question. As in "Who are you?"

The more we get to know our children as unique individuals, the better we will be able to plant them in the environments best suited for them to thrive.

Remember, disrupters are explosively creative. This is not a choice; it's how they were built. It's how they were wired. Therefore, if they don't fit the system in which your family operates, it's fair for them to ask whether the system can be changed.

When have you recently felt disrupted by someone from a younger generation?

Imagine you have a friend with a child who is a disrupter. What is one piece of parenting advice you would offer that friend?

For many people, including many who work through the material of this study guide, disruptive thinking is a new experience. It's a new approach to life. And one of the reliable by-products of "new" is fear. To try something new is to put ourselves in a position to feel afraid.

I hope you have put yourself in that position as you have studied this material. I hope you have made an effort to think disruptively and even live and act disruptively.

The reason I hope that with a fervency I find hard to express is because our culture desperately needs change. Your community desperately needs change. The old ways aren't working. The old systems need people to come in and burst the boundaries so we as a society can move in a new direction.

You have a part to play in that drama. Will you make the leap?

What are some examples of disruptive thinking you have experienced over the course of this study?

What is one of the main challenges you have experienced as you try to think more disruptively?

PRACTICE MAKES PERFECT

Setting goals is a useful skill for all people. The ability to identify what we want to run after is often the difference between those who run with purpose and those who run haphazardly. It's also a big reason why some people achieve their dreams and desires for success while many others do not.

So, spend a little time at the end of this study creating disruptive goals. Specifically, identify some ways you would like to think and live disruptively in the short term and in the long term. Once you've identified your personal goals using the prompts below, come together to discuss what it could look like to think disruptively as a group.

What is one situation in which you would like to demonstrate disruptive thinking in the next week?

What are some ways you would like to incorporate disruptive thinking into your life over the next year?

What is a pattern, system, or problem you would like to help disrupt in the next five years?

As a group, spend some time thinking disruptively about how your group operates. What are your goals? What do you want to accomplish as a community?

WRAP UP

Remember these truths as you conclude this discussion for session 6:

- Children and younger generations naturally seek to push against the systems in which they are raised. Sometimes it's the systems that need to change.

- Being a parent to a disruptive thinker likely means asking "Who are you?" more often than "Why are you like this?" or "Why did you…?"

- One of the ways to support and encourage young disrupters is to re-plant them in an environment where they can flourish.

- As you continue forward as a disruptive thinker, don't let yourself become settled or stagnant. Keep moving!